Simple Pleasures

A Reflection Journal of gratitude and positivity

By: Markisha Baker & Amada Bowers

GYST Publications

About the Authors

Markisha Baker:

Markisha Baker was born in Long Island, New York. She grew up in Raleigh, North Carolina where she began journaling at an early age. Throughout her formative years, Markisha grew a love for reading and writing. It is where she found solace while growing up in a large family. Her grandmother instilled in her the value of education, and after obtaining a Bachelor's and Master's degree, Markisha began her professional career and continued to journal through. Her love for journaling has been her sounding board, secret keeper, and therapy. When she isn't journaling or writing, she enjoys traveling, listening to music and spending time with family.

Amada Bowers:

Amada Bowers was born in Detroit, MI. where she spent most of her formative years. At the age of 16 she moved to Raleigh, North Carolina, where she planted her roots and established her home. After graduating high school, she had ambitions of becoming an entrepreneur with the hopes of owning her own salon. This goal came to fruition and Amada has worked in the beauty industry for over 20 years. She is the mother of two, Joshua and Bella. Being raised in both a large city setting, and the south has given her the ability to value different perspectives on life and the ability to see the beauty in our differences. She enjoys researching ideas and reading, and through this love of reading, she has found various motivational speakers, philosophers, and authors that has helped her journey through life.

Introduction

Welcome to the Simple Pleasures Journal where the idea is to take a few minutes of the day and focus on all that is good in your life. We are often boggled down with heavy and important things, so much so, that we forget to pay attention to the simple things. This journal was created with the idea that positive thoughts leads to a more positive life.

Markisha Baker and Amada Bowers are best friends who share the common joy of journaling. They decided to come together, share, and create something that they both love.

Take a few minutes of each day to reflect and remain grateful.

Enjoy the gems along the way!

We hope you enjoy this journal as much as we did creating it!

Date:

Today's Simple Pleasure:

"We are what we repeatedly do. Excellence, then is not an act but a habit" Aristotle, Philosopher

Date:

Today's Simple Pleasure:

"Everyone has the right to their opinion, and you have every right not to listen. Be confident in who you are, or you will be confused all the time" Mary J. Blige, Singer & Actress

Date:

Today's Simple Pleasure:

"*Be mindful of your self-talk. It is a conversation with the universe. You are a being, full of infinite possibilities! Focus your mind with positivity and you will have dictated the direction of your journey, your soul and your being, cascading in infinite abundance.*" Angie Karan, Blogger

Date:

Today's Simple Pleasure:

"Happiness is an inside job. Don't assign anyone else that much power over your life" Mandy Hale, Blogger & Author

Date:

Today's Simple Pleasure:

"You will always be too much of something for someone; too big, too loud, too soft, too edgy. If you round out your edges, you lose your edge. Apologize for mistakes. Apologize for unintentionally hurting someone – profusely. But don't apologize for being who you are." Danielle Laporte, Author

Date:

Today's Simple Pleasure:

"Worration will kill you" Annie Evelyn Baker, Markisha's grandma

Worration is defined as continuously stressing or worrying. So, stop stressing!!

Date:

Today's Simple Pleasure:

"Life is:
An opportunity; benefit from it.
A beauty; admire it.
A dream; realize it.
A challenge; meet it.
A duty; complete it.
A game; play it.
A promise; fulfill it.
Sorrow; overcome it.
A song; sing it.
A struggle; accept it.
A tragedy; confront it.
An adventure; dare it.
Luck, make it
Precious, don't destroy it.
Life is life, fight for it"
Mother Teresa, Missionary & Nun

Date:

Today's Simple Pleasure:

"Follow your bliss!" Omar Epps, Actor

Date:

Today's Simple Pleasure:

"Hold fast to dreams. For it dreams die, life is a broken-winged bird that cannot fly." Langston Hughes, Poet, Novelist, & Activist

Date:

Today's Simple Pleasure:

"I've learned that whenever I decide something with an open heart, I usually make the right decision." Dr. Maya Angelou, Poet, Author, & Activist

Date:

Today's Simple Pleasure:

"Don't try to lessen yourself for the world; let the world catch up to you." Beyoncé, Pop Star

Date:

Today's Simple Pleasure:

"You is smart. You is kind. You is important" Viola Davis, Actress, quote from 'The Help' movie

Date:

Today's Simple Pleasure:

"Be nice to yourself.... It's hard to be happy when someone is mean to you all the time" Christine Arylo, Author

Date:

Today's Simple Pleasure:

"Be kind with yourself when you experience apparent setbacks. They are a valuable part of life. See them as opportunities to reevaluate your goals and change your course of action as needed. Ask your inner wisdom and God to guide you." Mikaela Katherine Jones, Author

Date:

Today's Simple Pleasure:

"Life is all about balance. You don't always need to be getting stuff done. Sometimes it's perfectly okay, and absolutely necessary, to shut down, kick back, and do nothing" Lori Deschene, Author

Date:

Today's Simple Pleasure:

"Be empowered in the moment." Katura Devane, Financial Consultant & Dear Friend

Date:

Today's Simple Pleasure:

"There is no passion to be found in settling for a life that is less than the one you are capable of living." Nelson Mandela, Former President of South Africa, Philanthropist & Nobel Peace Prize recipient

Date:

Today's Simple Pleasure:

"In the sky above the clouds, there is a world peaceful where perspective and the one-ness of the divine of all is known. May you feel it all your days even on the ground" Author unknown.

Date:

Today's Simple Pleasure:

"Be open to it being way better than you imagined" Ralph Waldo Emerson, American Essayist

Date:

Today's Simple Pleasure:

"Happiness is like a kiss. You must share it to enjoy it."
Bernard Meltzer, **Radio Host**

Date:

Today's Simple Pleasure:

"Wherever you go, there you are!" Smokey Robinson, Singer and Songwriter

Date:

Today's Simple Pleasure:

"To read without reflecting is like eating without digesting."
Edmond Burke, British Statesman

Date:

Today's Simple Pleasure:

"Don't be a hard rock when you really are a gem" Lauryn Hill, singer

Date:

Today's Simple Pleasure:

"I am limited only by my vision of what is possible" Author Unknown

Date:

Today's Simple Pleasure:

"Life is like the ocean. It can be calm or still, and rough or rigid; but in the end, it's always beautiful." Author Unknown

Date:

Today's Simple Pleasure:

"It's faith in something and enthusiasm for something that makes a life worth living." Oliver Wendell Holmes, Author

Date:

Today's Simple Pleasure:

"So, if I'm looking up, don't mind me. But I can't be.... I just can't be down no more. And if you don't know where to find me; I'm out looking for the silver lining!" Jazmine Sullivan, Singer

Date:

Today's Simple Pleasure:

"The core of your true self is never lost. Let go of all the pretending and the becoming you've done just to belong. Curl up with your rawness and come home. You don't have to find yourself; you just have to let yourself in." D. Antoinette Foy, Writer

Date:

Today's Simple Pleasure:

"Be clean, both inside and out. Neither look up to the rich nor down on the poor. Lose if need be without squealing. Win without bragging. Always be considerate of women, children, and older people. Be too brave to lie. Be to generous to cheat. Take your share of the world and let others take theirs."
George Washington Carver, Inventor & Scientist

Date:

Today's Simple Pleasure:

"Life is an echo. What you send out, comes back. What you sow, you reap. What you give, you get. What you see in others, exists in you. Remember, life is an echo. It always gets back to you. So, give goodness." Zig Zaglar, Author & Motivational Speaker

Date:

Today's Simple Pleasure:

"I'll tell you what freedom is to me: No fear!" Nina Simone, Singer & Activist

Date:

Today's Simple Pleasure:

"Go confidently in the direction of your dreams and live the life that you've imagined" Henry David Thoreau, Essayist, Poet & Philosopher

Date:

Today's Simple Pleasure:

"May your choices reflect your hopes, not your fears." Nelson Mandela, Political Leader & Revolutionary

Date:

Today's Simple Pleasure:

"I alone cannot change the world, but I can cast a stone across the waters to create many ripples" Mother Teresa, Humanitarian

Date:

Today's Simple Pleasure:

"We do not learn from experience...we learn from reflecting on experience." John Dewey, Philosopher

Date:

Today's Simple Pleasure:

"Don't become too preoccupied with what is happening around you. Pay more attention to what is going on within you." Mary Frances Winters, CEO of The Winters Group, INC

Date:

Today's Simple Pleasure:

"Sweet words are easy to say, nice things are easy to buy, but good people are difficult to find...Life ends when you stop dreaming, hope ends when you stop believing, love ends when you stop crying, and friendship ends when you stop sharing." Mar Razalan, Blogger

Date:

Today's Simple Pleasure:

"Minds are like flowers, they open only when the time is right."
Stephen Richards, Author

Date:

Today's Simple Pleasure:

"Happiness is when what you think, what you say and what you do are in harmony." Mahatma Ghandi, Activist

Date:

Today's Simple Pleasure:

"The voice of beauty speaks softly; it creeps only into the most fully awakened souls." Neitzsche, Philosopher

Date:

Today's Simple Pleasure:

"A smile is a universal welcome." Mark Eastman, Author

Date:

Today's Simple Pleasure:

"Every adventure requires a first step." Cheshire Cat, Alice in Wonderland

Date:

Today's Simple Pleasure:

"Women need real moments of solitude and self-reflection to balance out how much of ourselves we give away." Barbara de Angelis, Author

Date:

Today's Simple Pleasure:

"You may shoot me with your words, you may cut me with your eyes, you may kill me with your hatefulness, but still, like air, I'll rise!" Maya Angelou, Poet

Date:

Today's Simple Pleasure:

"If you think trying is risky, wait till you get the bill for not trying." Jim Rohn, Entrepreneur

Date:

Today's Simple Pleasure:

"Just for the record darling, not all positive changes feel positive in the beginning." S.C. Lourie, Writer

Date:

Today's Simple Pleasure:

"If you don't heal what hurt you, you'll bleed on people who didn't cut you." Unknown

Date:

Today's Simple Pleasure:

"When you start seeing your worth, you'll find it harder to stay around people who don't." Unknown

Date:

Today's Simple Pleasure:

"Don't wait. Make your move now. The conditions will never be perfect. You'll never have enough time. You'll never have enough money. You'll never have enough knowledge. Do the best you can with what you have. The process of doing it will teach you everything you need to know." Paul Carrick Brunson, Author

Date:

Today's Simple Pleasure:

"A good teacher is like a candle. It consumes itself to light the way for others." Unknown

Date:

Today's Simple Pleasure:

"We unconsciously mirror and mimic who we're with. Align yourself with those that display behavior worth replicating." Ungenita Prevost, Leadership Expert

Date:

Today's Simple Pleasure:

"If you have nothing in life but a good friend, you are rich."
Michelle Kwan, Olympic Medalist

Date:

Today's Simple Pleasure:

"The kind of beauty I want most is the hard-to-get kind that comes from within — strength, courage, dignity." Ruby Dee, Actress

Date:

Today's Simple Pleasure:

"Once you've accepted your flaws, no one can use them against you." George R.R. Martin, Novelist

Date:

Today's Simple Pleasure:

"A beautiful woman delights the eye; a wise woman, the understanding; pure one, the soul." Minna Antrim, American Writer

Date:

Today's Simple Pleasure:

"The woman who does not require validation from anyone is the most feared individual." Mohadesa Nahumi, Social Scientist and Writer

Date:

Today's Simple Pleasure:

"Trendy is the last stage before tacky." Karl Lagerfeld, Designer

Date:

Today's Simple Pleasure:

"When you have confidence, you can have a lot of fun. And when you have fun, you can do amazing things." Joe Nameth, American Football Player and Actor.

Date:

Today's Simple Pleasure:

"What screws us up most in life is the picture in our head of how it is supposed to be." William Glasser, Psychiatrist

Date:

Today's Simple Pleasure:

"Your crown has been bought and paid for. All you must do is put it on." James Baldwin, Author and Activist

Date:

Today's Simple Pleasure:

"Life is a party. Dress like it." Audrey Hepburn, Actress

Date:

Today's Simple Pleasure:

"There are far better things ahead, than any we leave behind."
C.S. Lewis, British Writer

Date:

Today's Simple Pleasure:

"Risk it; go for it. Life always gives you another chance, another go at it. It's very important to take enormous risks."
Mary Quant, Fashion Designer

Date:

Today's Simple Pleasure:

"We cannot start over, but we can begin now and make a new ending." Zig Ziglar, Author and Motivational Speaker

Date:

Today's Simple Pleasure:

"To be beautiful means to be yourself. You don't need to be accepted by others. You need to accept yourself." Thich Nhat Hanh, Vietnamese Monk

Date:

Today's Simple Pleasure:

"Kill the part of you that believes it can't survive without someone else." Sade Andria Zabala, Author

Date:

Today's Simple Pleasure:

"Comparison is an act of violence against the self." Iyanla Vanzant, Author and Life Coach

Date:

Today's Simple Pleasure:

"She remembered who she was, and the game changed." Lala Deliah, Spiritual Writer

Date:

Today's Simple Pleasure:

"It is better to be hated for what you are than to be loved for something you are not." Andre Gide, Nobel Prize Author

Date:

Today's Simple Pleasure:

"You always gain by giving love." Reese Witherspoon, Actress

Date:

Today's Simple Pleasure:

"The is no charm equal to the tenderness of the heart." Jane Austen, Novelist

Date:

Today's Simple Pleasure:

"The most beautiful things in the world cannot be see or even touched. They must be touched with the heart." Helen Keller, Author and Political Activist

Date:

Today's Simple Pleasure:

"Life doesn't require that we are the best, only that we try our best." H. Jackson Brown, Jr., Author

Date:

Today's Simple Pleasure:

"A champion is defined not by their wins but how they recover when they fail." Serena Williams, Athlete and Entrepreneur

Date:

Today's Simple Pleasure:

"There are no limits to what you can accomplish, except the limits you place on your own thinking." Brain Tracy, Motivational Speaker

Date:

Today's Simple Pleasure:

"Keep your face always towards the sunshine and shadows will fall behind you." Walt Whitman, Poet

Date:

Today's Simple Pleasure:

"Don't be pushed around by the fears on your mind. Be led by the dreams in your heart." Roy T. Bennett, Author

Date:

Today's Simple Pleasure:

"Believe in yourself! Have faith in your abilities! Without a humble but responsible confidence in your own powers, you cannot be successful or happy." Norman Vincent Peale, Minister and Author

Date:

Today's Simple Pleasure:

"We encounter many defeats, but we must not be defeated."
Maya Angelou, Poet and Activist

Date:

Today's Simple Pleasure:

"Don't settle for average. Be your best to the moment. Then, whether it fails or succeeds at least you know you gave all you had. We need to live the best that's in us." Angela Bassett, Actress

Date:

Today's Simple Pleasure:

"My entire life can be described in one sentence. It didn't go as planned, and that's ok." Rachel Wolchin, Author

Date:

Today's Simple Pleasure:

"The words you speak become the house you live in." Hafiz, Poet

Date:

Today's Simple Pleasure:

"What you do today can improve your tomorrows." Ralph Marston, Football Player

Date:

Today's Simple Pleasure:

"Start where you are. Use what you have. Do what you can."
Author Ash, Tennis Player

Date:

Today's Simple Pleasure:

"Your talent is God's gift to you. What you do with it is your gift back to God." Leo Buscaglia, Author

Date:

Today's Simple Pleasure:

"Good, better, best. Never let it rest; 'til your good is better and your better is best." St. Jerome, Priest

Date:

Today's Simple Pleasure:

"The Key to growth is acknowledging your fear of the unknown and jumping anyway." Jen Sincero, Author & Success Coach

Date:

Today's Simple Pleasure:

"Take a deep breath, pick yourself up, dust yourself off, and start all over again." Frank Sinatra, Singer

Date:

Today's Simple Pleasure:

"I never lose. I either win or learn." Nelson Mandela, Former President of South Africa

Date:

Today's Simple Pleasure:

"There is no failure except in no longer trying." Elbert Hubbard, Writer & Artist

Date:

Today's Simple Pleasure:

"Whether you think that you can, or that you can't, you are usually right." Henry Ford, Founder of Ford Motor Company

Date:

Today's Simple Pleasure:

"Be teachable. You are not always right!" Unknown

Date:

Today's Simple Pleasure:

"One of the lessons that I grew up with was to always stay true to yourself and never let what somebody else says distract you from your goals. So, when I hear about negative and false attacks, I really don't invest any energy in them because I know who I am." Michelle Obama, Former U.S. First Lady

Date:

Today's Simple Pleasure:

"If she's amazing, she won't be easy. If she's easy, she won't be amazing. If she's worth it, you won't give up. If you give up, you're not worthy." Bob Marley, Singer

Date:

Today's Simple Pleasure:

"Once you know who you are, you don't have to worry anymore." Nikki Giovanni, Poet

Date:

Today's Simple Pleasure:

"Turn your wounds into wisdom." Oprah Winfrey, Media Executive, Actress, and Philanthropist

Date:

Today's Simple Pleasure:

"The future belongs to those who prepare for it today."
Malcolm X, Minister and Human Rights Activist

Date:

Today's Simple Pleasure:

"You must never be fearful about what you are doing when it is right." Rosa Parks, Civil Rights Activist

Date:

Today's Simple Pleasure:

"A people without the knowledge of their past history, origin, and culture is like a tree without roots." Marcus Garvey, Political Leader

Date:

Today's Simple Pleasure:

"*The great difficulty lies in trying to transpose last night's moment to a day which has no knowledge of it.*" Zora Neale Hurston, Author

Date:

Today's Simple Pleasure:

"Change will not come it we wait for some other person or some other time. We are the ones we've been waiting for. We are the change that we seek." Barack Obama, 44th U.S. President

Date:

Today's Simple Pleasure:

"Greatness can be captured in one word: Lifestyle. Life is God's gift to you. Style is what you make of it." Mae Jemison, Engineer, Physician and NASA Astronaut

Date:

Today's Simple Pleasure:

"Never be limited by other people's limited imaginations."
Mae Jemison, NASA Astronaut

Date:

Today's Simple Pleasure:

"You've got to learn to leave the table when love is no longer being served." Nina Simone, Musician & Activist

Date:

Today's Simple Pleasure:

"I am always ok, because I am with me!" Tracee Ellis Ross, Actress

Date:

Today's Simple Pleasure:

"You have seen your own strength. You have seen your own beauty. You have seen your golden wings. Why do you worry?"
Rumi, Poet

Date:

Today's Simple Pleasure:

"Today you are you, that is truer than true. There is no one alive that is youer than you." Dr. Suess, Author

Acknowledgements

We would like to thank everyone that we have met on this journey called life. Your presence in our lives has given us quotes to live by, daily mantras, and gems that we cherish!

We dedicate this journal to the dreamers, thinkers, and knowledge seekers.

Made in the USA
Columbia, SC
26 October 2020